LIBRARY OF
INTERIORS

Living Rooms

LIBRARY OF
INTERIORS

Living Rooms

Amanda Harling

Trafalgar Square Publishing

To M and M

First published in United States of America in 1996 by
Trafalgar Square Publishing
North Pomfret
Vermont 05053

Printed and bound in Spain by Bookprint

Copyright © Pavilion Books 1996
Photographs copyright see page 94
Designed by Peter Bennett
Picture research by Emily Hedges

The moral right of the publisher has been asserted.

ISBN: 1–57076–051–9
Library of Congress Catalog Card Number: 95–62179

Typeset in Gill Sans Medium.

10 9 8 7 6 5 4 3 2 1

Contents

Introduction

Successful living rooms come in all shapes, sizes and colors – as can be seen in the pages

of this book. Yet one factor they all have in common is the sense of

comfort. Imbued with vitality and warmth, they are the sort of

rooms that one longs to find at the end of a long journey.

Pleasing to the eye and in their own small way uplifting to the spirit.

There are philistines who claim to be oblivious to their domestic surroundings, but most of

us are acutely aware of whether or not we like the design of a room. One only has to think of the

vast budgets that interior designers have at their disposal to realize that the business of making people feel

comfortable and happy is taken very seriously indeed by those whose livelihoods depend on it; hoteliers,

restaurateurs and club owners spring to mind. Fortunately most of us are in the position of having only our own

modest house, cottage or apartment to do up but the principle remains the same – the more inviting and

commodious a room, the more it is enjoyed – by owners and guests alike.

Good interior design is not dependent on money. Having been involved in the world of

design and decoration for most of my life, I have been privileged to see within innumerable

private homes – some vast, some minuscule. While many of those verging on the palatial

have clearly had a king's ransom lavished upon them, there is never any guarantee that these glitzy houses will be

deemed worthy of being written about or photographed – acres of marble and gold taps are not what magazine

editors are looking for. Homes that have been decorated with verve and imagination are infinitely preferable and they

are undoubtedly the most difficult to find. These examples of stylish interior decoration are even more difficult to define. They have an immediate visual impact: sometimes due to grandeur but more frequently as a result of a unique fusion of color, scale and comfort.

Over the past ten years or so there has been a phenomenal growth of interest in interior design. Whereas it was formerly considered to be the domain of the wealthy, home interest magazines and television programs have done much to increase the general awareness of design for the home. Terence Conran and Laura Ashley were also hugely instrumental, in their very different ways, in bringing style to main street.

Large department stores devote ever-increasing amounts of floor space to furniture and home accessories and they can be an excellent source of ideas and inspiration. Don't limit your window-shopping to the large stores, as the small specialist retailer will have a much wider range to choose from and should offer a far greater level of expertise when it comes to advising you on design as well as technical details.

Blending the disparate elements of interior design into a home that reflects your individuality is an exciting challenge. On the following pages you will find rooms decorated in a wide range of styles, which will help you to define your own personal preferences. You will also come across numerous inventive ideas that can be adapted to your own particular circumstances. The extensive directory at the back of the book should be of help in the search for suppliers, manufacturers and retailers of decorative furniture, fabrics and accessories.

Anyone in possession of a credit card can furnish a living room, but to instill character and individuality requires

something more – confidence in your own inimitable taste. You can of course opt out of the challenge of doing it all

yourself by engaging an interior designer. But why miss out on the fun? Take on the project yourself and become

immersed in the irresistible world of color, design and decoration. It is, after all, a subject that has engrossed the

civilized world for generation after generation.

Having confidence in your own judgement is essential. A wonderful idea

can so easily be diluted into pallid compromise by those who don't

share your vision. Study books on decoration. Look at

paintings and notice how they are framed. Visit not only museums but the great houses

in your area and beyond. Compare the work of interior designers. Analyze those features

which you think make or break a room. Build up a file of magazine and newspaper cuttings that you

find particularly interesting and inspiring. If there's an aspect of design that you become passionate about, think

about incorporating it into the decoration of the room (as has the owner of the cottage illustrated on page 37). It

will prove to be enormous fun and who knows, you might soon find yourself inundated with commissions from

admiring friends.

While some of the living rooms shown in these pages are the work of professional

interior designers, many have been created by their accomplished but entirely amateur

owners. The methods with which these imaginative and individual rooms have been put

together varies enormously, as do characteristics such as architectural style, size, layout

and so on. Though a sense of traditionalism is evident in most of the rooms, it is traditionalism with a distinctly

contemporary edge. There are absolutely no museum pieces and no stately homes – but over a hundred very

comfortably lived-in rooms – each and every one a source of inspiration.

Style

Deciding upon a style of decoration that is both appropriate for the room and pleasing to the eye is the most important part of any interior design project. Careful consideration must be given to this critical aspect right from the beginning, as it is not something that can easily or cheaply be rectified halfway through the exercise. Though it can be tempting to take advantage of a bargain, it is generally a better idea to wait until you know roughly what look you are aiming for before you venture forth armed with a check book. While it's easy to relegate an unsuitable item of clothing to the local charity shop, getting rid of an ill-chosen suite of furniture can prove rather more problematical.

In these stylistically anarchic times, choosing a style or styles of decoration can be a bewildering process. Set aside time to work out what types of interiors you find particularly pleasing. It might help to jot down a few notes with a description of your ideal room. Do you like the sparseness of minimal decoration – white walls, little furniture and a

feeling of space, or do you feel happier surrounded with color and pattern? Perhaps you find yourself attracted to the clean, uncompromising lines of modern furniture, or maybe you feel that a combination of antique, contemporary and ethnic pieces holds more appeal.

The architectural period of the building often provides a useful reference point from which to start planning. An existing feature of a room, such as an inglenook fireplace, might suggest the gleam of dark furniture and richly textured fabrics. A solid wood-block floor might point you in the direction of a more contemporary style where natural materials and neutral colors work so well together. While there is no reason to

stick rigidly to that period's style of decoration, it often helps to bear in mind the nature and scale of the building when deciding what sort of furniture to choose, leading to a harmonious final result. Developing a basic knowledge of general decorative styles will prove invaluable, enabling you to make informed decisions regarding the choice of fabrics, colors and furniture in addition to the innumerable other details that contribute to the making of a successful living room. It also prevents basic mistakes being made, such as introducing inappropriate materials and designs into period rooms.

Traditional-style rooms come in many guises but the principal elements — fabrics, wall colors, furniture and accessories — are based on period designs. There has never been such a wide variety of merchandise available in as many period styles as there is now. Having settled on a style of decoration that you think is suitable for your home and your way of life, don't feel duty-bound to throw out existing furniture even if it is of the wrong period. Furniture has always been passed down through the generations and it is through combining furniture, paintings and fabrics of different periods that some of the most successful rooms evolve. A particular architectural or decorative style can be created in any number of ways — using the wall color, the fabric design, the period details such as panelling, window design, fireplace design or a curtain treatment. While authentic period pieces add character to the room, think carefully about the seating — oak settles may be in keeping with sixteenth and seventeenth-century style but they are not comfortable.

Similarly, Georgian sofas are beautiful but can be unyielding and rather formal in appearance. A contemporary sofa

made in a traditional style will certainly prove more comfortable, and when covered in a fabric of the chosen period it

will help to contribute a sense of period style to the room. Learn to identify the particular characteristics of the period

you're interested in, so that when you come to buy furniture you will be able to assess immediately whether the piece

 is of the period and style that you're looking for. The advantage of this approach can be

seen around some of the best dinner tables: sets of period dining chairs

are notoriously expensive but it is often possible to pick up a fine

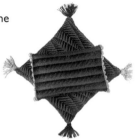

single chair for a modest outlay. A collection of chairs of

roughly the same period, perhaps differing slightly in tone, style and size, will co-exist quite

happily round the table, whereas the effect of a group of widely differing styles is confusing.

When embarking upon the decoration of any period property, the key point to remember is whether

the style is appropriate or not. To install Corinthian columns in a cottage, or replace sash windows with aluminum

frames would be sacrilegious. Many people are now replacing architectural details such as cornices, deep

baseboards, panelled doors and fireplaces which were ripped out in the decades after the Second World War when

modernism ruled over aesthetic considerations. It is now generally accepted that the basic architectural

 proportions of Georgian, Victorian and Edwardian houses had been refined to a point

which is difficult to improve upon. This appreciation of heritage has even been extended to

paint manufacturers, who now go to great pains to reproduce authentic period colors.

Even the earlier types of paint, such as distemper, are once again proving popular.

Climate strongly influences our way of life – pale, watery daylight is much better suited to interiors furnished

with subdued and muted colors. Even in these days of central heating and air conditioning, most of us still consider

an open fire to be a highly desirable feature in living rooms. Insulated windows and storm windows have largely done away with the need for the insulating qualities of heavy interlined curtains, but the traditional style remains a

favorite and will be with us for the forseeable future. However, the frilled, flounced extravaganzas that billowed into

fashion a decade or so ago have now given way to less grandiose window treatments that are more in keeping with

the general movement towards a simpler, 'less is more' lifestyle. We still love to mix the exotic with the antique.

The English-country-house look partly owes its origins to early travelers and traders.

Lacquerwork, ceramics and porcelain from China, cottons and silks from India, rugs from

the Middle East, paintings, sculpture and fine furniture from Italy and France – all were

imported in vast quantities during the seventeenth, eighteenth and nineteenth centuries,

leading to permanent changes in our notions of style.

Over the last hundred years or so, design movements such as Arts and Crafts, Art Deco and Modernism have

strongly influenced interior design. Currently, as the vogue for simpler interiors continues, the work of innovative

13

young designers is finding an appreciative market.

Bearing in mind the uses to which the room will be put helps to define a style that will be

pleasing as well as practical. If small children are likely to be around, you will probably do

better to postpone the use of finer fabrics until the danger of self-expression with crayons

and paint is past. If you propose to use the room for work as well as play, take into account at

the initial stages the requirement for a desk or table adequate for your needs. Trying to fit in a large

piece of furniture at a later stage often proves unsatisfactory, as the balance of the room is destroyed.

The living rooms shown in the following section are furnished and decorated in a wide

variety of styles ranging from rustic informality to stark minimalism. All are highly

individual and resist strict categorization, but in each case the finished result successfully

enhances the characteristics of that particular room.

Although informal and unpretentious, this living room is decorated with great individual style, redolent of a Gothic extravaganza. The fireside chair and the chest of drawers are of different though complementary styles, ensuring that the room is not just a pastiche. The fireplace, with its decorative elements highlighted in strawberry-red paint, sets the tone for this unusual and colorful interpretation of Gothic style.

The sculptural qualities of wrought iron are a strong decorative feature in this contemporary living room. In addition to the staircase, which rises through the house, a low glass-topped coffee table is designed along the same spare lines. White walls and a well-upholstered white sofa recall the all-white rooms created by the Edwardian decorator Syrie Maugham, but in this case accents of strong blues and yellows have been introduced. The result is uncluttered and elegant.

A contemporary interpretation of a classical Georgian interior is illustrated in this strongly colored blue and yellow sitting room. The fine proportions of the room are emphasized by dividing the walls into symmetrical panels and highlighting the moldings in white paint. A yellow of such strength would not have been used during the period, but, teamed with the black fireplace and the bright blue of the sofas and rug, the choice appears entirely appropriate.

Some rooms are clearly and unashamedly dedicated to luxurious comfort, and this certainly is such a room. The rich cream color of the walls, curtains, sofa and carpet emphasizes the feeling of space. The note of luxury is established at the moment of entry by the vision of extravagant nineteenth-century-style swags and tails of the curtain treatment for the wide bay window. Opulent and costly in this case, such a style is not beyond even quite modest budgets.

Left: A mixture of textures, patterns and soft, muted colors gives this room a cozy, Victorian feeling. The comfort and display associated with traditional living rooms is manifest — a deep-seated chintz-covered armchair mixes happily with a more rugged pair covered in leather. Above: This beautiful, nineteenth-century room has been given an open, contemporary feeling by painting the walls a pale hyacinth blue and leaving the windows free of curtains.

Left: The color combination of blue and cream is typical of traditional Scandinavian decoration, and the style of this living room is similarly cool, classical and restrained. The *trompe-l'oeil* panels on the walls add interest and highlight the fine architectural proportions of the room. Above: By providing little in the way of distraction, muted shades of cream and white have been used to create a sophisticated setting for this beautifully displayed but understated collection of oriental artefacts.

Decorative textiles have been used to great effect in this warm and welcoming country living room. With so many gorgeous patterns to study, one is scarcely aware of the white painted walls and ceiling, but it is that plain background that stops the room from appearing claustrophobic. Each and every pattern used in this living room is different, but the final result is far from confusing to the eye, due to the tonal similarity of the colors.

There is nothing precious about the decoration of this country living room. In order to increase the feeling of space in what was formerly a cramped, poky couple of rooms, the original boxed-in staircase was removed and replaced with one of a more open design. White-painted walls and ceiling reflect light into the room and provide an uncluttered background for the patterned blue and white fabrics used for upholstery and curtains.

Left: A simple brushwood garland seen hanging above the wood-burning stove sums up the charm and character of a cozy, unpretentious country living room. Above: Equipped with a practical wood-burning stove, the large fireplace is the natural focal point in this informal country sitting room. Casually but confidently thrown together, it is furnished with a well-worn collection of antiques mixed with contemporary paintings and ceramics. A kelim rug adds a vibrant note of color to the flagstone floor.

Top: Austerity allied with comfort is the keynote of this highly mannered room with its oriental overtones and eye-catching elements. The simple yet rather grand bureau with its quietly spectacular cupboard is set between a pair of handsome Indian paintings and a boldly contemporary Chinese folding screen. Above: The pale airy sitting room of this 1830s house is furnished with a cherrywood table and bookcase made by the owner.

An interesting room which combines the best elements of tradition and modernism. At first glance this appears to be a rather austere living room, an impression deriving from the unusual design of the sofa, which makes its own link between Victorian deep-cushioned comfort and the spare modern lines of the frame – a modernism that is echoed in the shape of the coffee table. A pair of Regency elbow chairs adds to the duality of the overall concept in the same way as the softly gathered curtains.

24

Property developer Sara May converted a former
office unit into a compact one-bedroomed home. The
focal point of the plain, white-painted room was created
by the hanging, a vibrantly colored painting by Mark
Wigan in the center of the main wall. The highly eclectic
mix of contemporary, antique and ethnic furniture and
accessories subsequently chosen for the room reflect
the colors in the painting. A sense of order is imposed
by the arrangement of the furniture.

A serenely splendid Regency sofa upholstered in mattress ticking is the focal point in this symmetrical arrangement of furniture in the living room of an 1840s London house. The pale buff color of the walls was picked from a color in the pretty, striped curtains bought at a London antique market. A pair of strikingly modern low-voltage standard lamps casts light at either end of the sofa, and the portrait cushions add an amusing contemporary touch.

Below: Windows can be the most assertive element in any interior setting, and certain windows – from Gothic to great modern spaces – can become arbiters of the decoration within. This is especially true of windows that offer unusual or even spectacular vistas beyond – as seen here. For such breathtaking scenes, the 'less is more' philosophy has substantial appeal. Right: Minimal chic – a chair, a desk, a window, and little else except light, space and the warm color of a wood-strip floor.

Color, Pattern

Color has the most profound influence on the atmosphere of any room, but with a vast

array of papers, paints and fabrics to choose from it is a subject that can

seem bewilderingly complex. Reaction to color, combinations of

color, patterns and texture deeply affect the way we feel.

Some make us feel secure, others make us initially optimistic but pall after a short time.

There seem to be innumerable variations with few set rules. Some people have a natural eye for

the fine gradations of color, others can barely detect the difference between yellow and ochre. Close

observation and experience are invaluable in taming this most subjective of areas. Certain colors and patterns are

associated with specific periods and styles of decoration. In many cases this is due to the availability of pigments at

the time in question. Until the middle of the nineteenth century, when a great many of the more difficult colors

were made synthetically, the range was fairly limited. Moreover, the quality of commercially available pigments was

nowhere near as dependable as we have come to take for granted today. The result,

however, was often to produce the most subtle and natural texture full of imperfections,

which gave such character to these period decorative schemes – something that no

modern vinyl or latex can achieve despite its stability, washability and durability.

During the sixteenth century, the predominant colors used in tapestries and crewel-work were the muted shades

of blues, greens, earthy reds and ochres obtained through using natural dyes. Rooms would have been wood-panelled

or decorated with patterns or images painted onto roughly plastered walls. Rich, jewel-like colors, such as deep

& Texture

reds, blues and greens, suited the ornate grandeur of the baroque style in the latter part of

the seventeenth century. During the early part of the eighteenth century the French rococo

style was associated with pale pinks, blues, yellows and greens and the plentiful use of

mirror and gilt, further adding to the effect of lightness and elegance. Also typical of that

time were *toile de Jouy* fabrics with their amusing depictions of bucolic country scenes. The Regency period, which

broadly spans the end of the eighteenth century and the beginning of the nineteenth century, was characterized by

forthright colors often combined in stripes. In particular this period will always be associated with the color red,

which was extensively used to convey the luxury and liveliness of the times. Decorative painting such as

marbling and graining was very much in vogue and the relative cheapness of its execution, in

comparison with the wonderful richness of color and texture it produced, made it

extremely popular. Well-to-do Victorians considered themselves pillars of a solid and

respectable Establishment, and their homes reflected this gravitas. Furniture and fabrics of a

frivolous nature were consigned to the attic, and reception rooms became repositories for vast

amounts of dark-brown furniture and heavily fringed, somber fabrics. The intricate and beautifully balanced designs

of William Morris, the leading exponent of the Arts and Crafts Movement, are still

produced – ideal for creating an instant impression of late-Victorian style. The interest in

period style continues unabated – wallpaper and fabric manufacturers add new designs to

their collections each season, but the theme or principal motif is more often than not adapted from a classical or traditional design. Some companies produce no new designs, merely re-coloring patterns

from their archive collection to fit in with the current vogue. One constant running through all these periods is the

fact that white has rarely been used in the decoration of interiors, with the exception of ceilings, which were often

tinted with red or blue anyway. However, during the latter half of this century, especially in the field of

contemporary design, white has become much more popular.

The direction in which your living room faces will have an important

bearing on which color you choose for the walls. Rooms with a

northerly aspect often appear to be lacking in warmth, so

you might compensate for this by using a sunny yellow or ochre. Cooler, lighter colors

such as off-whites, pale greens, yellows and blues can work especially well in rooms facing

south and enjoying plentiful natural light. Attempting to make small, dark rooms appear lighter

through the use of white or off-white is generally a mistake; the lack of natural light will result in the room feeling

merely dull and colorless. An alternative course of action would be to use a deep red or green to imbue the room

with a sense of warmth and drama. Add bookshelves, good lighting and strongly colored curtains, and you have the

makings of cozy library-cum-living room.

It is a far easier task to match wall color to fabric than the other way round. Study the

constituent colors of the fabric closely; you might find that one of the less dominant

colors proves ideal for the walls. Curtains and walls are always adjacent; when the colors

bear a close relationship to each other the effect is generally pleasantly harmonious. An

increasing number of specialist companies now produce ranges of historically accurate colors, using traditional

methods and materials to achieve an authentic finish. They may be more expensive but, although similar colors are

to be found in mass produced modern paints, they lack the depth of color and inimitable texture of paint produced using traditional methods and natural pigments. By using broken color it is possible to add a softer, more natural appearance to wall surfaces and furniture. In nature, uniform coloration is a totally unknown phenomenon. If a child is asked to paint a tree, the leaves are always depicted as one shade of green and the trunk is brown. In reality, however a leaf is many shades of green, just as the trunk is rarely brown but a mixture of greys and greens. If the

subject of decorative paint finishes is new to you, try experimenting with sample-size pots of two similar shades of the same color. You will be amazed at the sense of depth and movement that can be added to a flat surface by applying the paint in different ways. For instance, by painting a thinned-down mixture of one color over the other, a two-tone effect is immediately produced. Or use a brush to drag down vertically for a gently striated look. There are numerous books available on the subject that will explain the processes involved in more detail.

It is important not to underestimate the significance of texture in the overall decorative scheme. Without

the interplay of light and shadow on a variety of surfaces an otherwise stunning room can appear lifeless and dull. Sisal, coir and jute floor coverings with their rich textural qualities look equally at home in traditional and contemporary settings. For those who prefer the softness of conventional carpet, several manufacturers now produce ranges that imitate the appearance of coir matting.

Rugs and dhurries can be used to introduce an element of pattern as well as texture and are also useful for the way that they help to define a particular part of a room, particularly in large rooms with sections used for different purposes – such as the fireside or the seating area. The textural qualities of different fabrics varies enormously – as can be seen if you compare the effect of sunlight shining on the surface of silk, cotton and velvet – and can have a significant influence on the appearance of a room.

Below: The owner of this house used primary colors of red, yellow and blue to make a bold statement in this handsomely proportioned living room. Sunny yellow walls and the russety tones of the wooden floorboards ensure that the room glows with warmth on even the gloomiest winter day. Plain white curtains add to the feelling of space by reflecting light back into the room. Right: Another view of this colorful room furnished in an eclectic mixture of styles.

The combination of color, texture and pattern convey an atmosphere of cozy sophistication in this sitting room containing a fine collection of satinwood Biedermeier furniture. The light sheen of the lustrous ochre-colored wall finish provides an effective backdrop for the pictures, ornaments and red and ochre curtain fabric. As always, the natural texture and color of coir floor covering proves the perfect foil for the patterns and colors of an oriental rug.

A wall finish in tones of pale golden-yellow distemper adds a sense of warmth to this formal drawing room. The other colors in the room are based on those of the woven green, cream and red fabric chosen to cover the sofas and the pair of boldly striped silk cushions, giving the room a striking, yet homogeneous look. Plain, undyed silk taffeta curtains are trimmed with tassels and braid in deep red, a color combination echoed in the bordered rug that defines the seating area.

Blue and yellow is a classic color combination, which works well in this cozy, unpretentious country living room where the cool tones of the carpet and sofa are balanced by the deep egg-yolk yellow walls. A collection of silhouettes hung in a symmetrical arrangement to one side of the stone fireplace adds interest to the room, as do the antique needlework cushions. The mantelpiece arrangement, though simple, is beautifully balanced, with the *trompe l'oeil* adding a decorative touch.

Right: A rich mix of Mediterranean colors creates a feeling of *joie de vivre* in this airy apartment. Lofty, off-white walls provide a muted backdrop for hot spicy shades of reds, pinks and terracotta. Luminous lilac blue cotton covering the sofa and chair adds a sharp note of contrast. Below: Though refurbished on a limited budget, the style and sophistication of this room are largely due to the bold use of color. Brilliant bright green walls emphasize the outline of a curvaceous purple sofa.

The paintings of Bloomsbury Group artists Vanessa Bell, Duncan Grant and Roger Fry inspired the owner of this country cottage to take up the paintbrush himself — with dazzling results. A total disregard for convention has resulted in a series of informal, colorful rooms. The manner in which each of the walls has been roughly painted in a different color and then hung with a profusion of prints, drawings and collages cleverly obscures the lack of architectural details.

This living room illustrates how pale colors can work well in rooms blessed with lofty proportions and plenty of natural light. Muted shades of cream, fawn and white are contrasted by the ebonized Regency dining chairs, the splendidly ornate gilt mirror and the marble fireplace. The gently gathered plain cream curtains soften the outline of the two floor-to-ceiling windows and, by being tied back into graceful folds, they avoid making the windows appear too austere.

A color combination of cream and pink was chosen for this country living room. The room receives little natural light but the atmosphere created by the soft, warm colors and the muted patterns is restful and welcoming. Contrast and interest are provided by the pine fireplace and the unusual *faux*-bamboo pedimented bookcase, which fits neatly into the broad, arched alcove. The delicately pleated silk lampshades add to the room's feminine appeal.

The rich red-and-gold color scheme used in this apartment detracts from the modest dimensions of the room. Inspiration for the unusual wall finish came from the patterned French curtain fabric — a burgundy and ochre wool weave acquired at an antique fair. The walls were painted in a gold base color, followed by two shades of red. After each stage the surface was rubbed down in order to remove some of the paint and create an impression of texture and depth.

Far from being oppressive, the deep red wallpaper and red lampshades give this tiny living room-cum-library an atmosphere of warmth and merriment. Though furnished very much in the traditional manner with mahogany bookcases, wing chairs, club fender and ancestral portrait, the effect is lightened by a contemporary upholstery fabric boldly checked in tones of red and yellow. The pale, natural colors of the carpet and the patterned rug also give the room a more modern feel.

By using a color scheme based predominantly on shades of earthy reds and browns, harmony of color, pattern and texture has been skilfully achieved in this European living room. The gradation of brown ranges from the deep conker of the window frames and door, and the tawny variations in the wood floor, to the pale tan of the patterned wallpaper. The sofa, covered in a fine red-and-cream stripe, is framed by the stronger colors and design of the curtain fabric.

Since Georgian times, dark red has been considered an excellent color against which to hang fine paintings – in this case of equestrian subjects. In this comfortable, traditionally furnished living room there is a strong contrast between the deep raspberry-red wall finish and the pristine white paintwork of the arched alcove and the white marble fire surround. The sofa upholstered in cream striped fabric is bedecked with a colorful array of cushions, providing yet more contrast.

The walls of this musical living room have been painted a soft shade of hyacinth blue, highlighted by a chalky white ceiling and dado. Although blue is generally thought of as being a cold color, this shade with its hint of violet gives the room an air of tranquillity rather than coolness. The russet tones of the oak strip-floor add warmth, as do the earthy colors seen in the oriental rug. The highly polished black surface of the grand piano adds to the understated sense of individuality.

The pale grey-green walls of this uncluttered modern apartment would seem cold if not balanced by the earthy tones of yellow ochre and burnt sienna used for the upholstery of the armchairs. The expanse of oak strip- flooring adds more warmth to the color scheme, as do the exposed wood of the window frames and the slats of the blinds. The gleaming brasswork set into the antique chest adds a decorative touch to this restrained, though colorful interior.

Left: Age and climate have softened the dramatic effect of this unusual color combination consisting of upper walls painted an intense turquoise and lower walls palest blue. Although this simply furnished 'sala de estar' is in an old Spanish house, the strong colors could look equally striking in a more northerly climate. Above: The old saying 'red and green should never be seen' is proved wrong in this case. A fiery red carpet adds theatrical strength to the celadon green walls and the floral curtains.

Right: The height of this unusual, vaulted sitting room is emphasized by painting the area above the picture rail white, while the pale shade of green chosen for the lower part of the walls provides an ideal background color for the decorative pair of Chinese watercolors on the far wall. Warmth and pattern have been introduced by way of the richly patterned fabric on the sofa. Below: Yards of flowered chintz stand out against the plain pastel walls and carpet in this softly colored country-style room.

Space

Whatever the size of your home, you will want to make the most of the space. Your first priority therefore is to make an accurate floorplan. Without one, every decision you make will be based on guesswork, inevitably leading to a series of unsatisfactory compromises on both the design and technical aspects of the project. Even the mathematically challenged should be able, with the help of a friend holding the other end of the tape, to measure the length, breadth and height of the room. Draw a rough sketch showing the general shape of the room and enter the measurements on the sketch. Measure every architectural detail in the room – height and width of fireplace, alcove sizes, chair-rail height, the width and direction in which doors open – it's often possible that just by re-hanging a door on the opposite side, 30in or more of wall space can be gained.

Then, having invested in a scale ruler, make a carefully measured plan and elevations of the area. Interior designers

generally use a scale of 1:50, which is considered adequate since it allows space to show the exact position of small details such as power points and light switches. Once you are satisfied that the plan is accurate, make several photocopies. They will prove invaluable, as you can supply the plumber, electrician and carpenter with an exact plan of where you want things positioned. Don't be tempted to leave the decisions up to them for their only concern is to do the job quickly, get paid and move onto the next one.

Once the scale floorplan and elevations are complete you will be able to calculate how best to use the available

floor and wall area of the room. Any furniture that you already have should be measured

so that scale cut-outs can be made; then, putting out of your mind how the room was

arranged previously, move the symbols around on the plan until you find the position that

suits you and the layout of the room. You will find that various configurations of furniture

are possible in even the smallest of living rooms.

Even if you think you have plenty of space, think long and hard before crowding your living room with furniture.

A massive living room suite might look great in a furniture store the size of an aircraft hangar, but a conventional

living room will be swamped by several items of furniture covered in identical fabric. You could start off

with the sofa and see whether chairs in a different style, covered in a complementary fabric,

would look less imposing.

Begin by deciding where the seating area should be. If you have a fireplace, the chances

are that you will want to locate sofas and chairs within its vicinity. Then work out what other

activities need to be planned for. Do you plan to use the room for work or study? Should it be child-

proof with space for high-spirited fun and games? Do you need shelf space for books and ornaments? Will there be

a television in the room? Do you need good daylight for needlework or painting?

Taking these requirements into account at the planning stage helps you to organize the

space so that the room can accommodate its multifarious roles in a functional, orderly

manner. Once the seating plan has been decided upon, this will dictate the positions of things such as power and lighting points, wall light heights, radiator locations and television socket – all vital

information that is needed before decoration can begin. Also bear in mind how much floor space an average-sized

person needs to maneuver between pieces of furniture. Failure to plan leads to chaotic, uncomfortable

arrangements where valuable floor space is lost unnecessarily to bulky afterthoughts. Incorporating storage space

 into the living room from the outset will pay dividends for years to come. Personal

possessions and general family clutter accumulate at an alarming rate even

in the tidiest of homes, but if they are tucked away out of sight the

room doesn't become dominated by the unsightly piles of

toys, games and videos that are part of everyday life. Alcoves either side of the

chimney often make ideal combined storage and display areas. Turn the lower part into

cupboards and use the upper section for books and ornaments. If the alcove recess is deep enough,

use the space for the television and stereo equipment.

Try to avoid one seating area becoming over-sized. While three-seater sofas are proportionally correct for

larger rooms, bear in mind that three people will rarely feel comfortable sitting cheek by jowl in a row, unless they

already know each other well and are relaxed in each other's company. As a general rule, seating more than eight

people in one group tends to make the room feel rather like a waiting room, so if you

have a spacious room, organizing the seating into more intimate groups will create a

cozier atmosphere. Such arrangements, where people can move easily from one group

to another, are ideal for informal family gatherings – grown-ups can chat amongst

themselves, while keeping an eye on the antics across the room!

Large living rooms lend themselves perfectly to multi-functional roles. If you work at home, turn one half of the

room into an office-cum-library with bookshelves and cupboards lining the walls, while the other half can be kept for the relaxed entertaining of friends. Use a central table as a desk, which, when occasion demands, can also double as a dining table. Alternatively, if space allows, try placing a table between the two halves of the room. Loaded with books and flowers, the table will mark the division between the seating areas, as well as providing a surface for homework or letter-writing.

If the living room is to be multi-functional, make sure the furniture is, too. Invest in a desk fitted with filing drawers, so that when the working day is over papers can be stored away. Upholstered stools fitted with an integral storage compartment for files and papers can double up as coffee tables, while purpose-built circular chipboard tables will conceal a television and video when covered with a tablecloth.

Certain styles of furniture appear to take up less space than they actually do. Wicker sofas and chairs provide a light, natural-looking alternative to conventional upholstery. Stacking and folding chairs are other useful allies in the quest for space. Other space-enhancing tricks include using the transparent, reflective qualities of glass wherever practicable. Glass-top occasional tables detract little from the spaciousness of a room, as do glass-top coffee and dining tables and glass-stemmed lights.

A classic method of increasing the sense of light and space is to use only white or pale colors throughout the room. In theory this works well, but only in rooms that already benefit from plentiful natural light. In practice, no amount of white paint will transform a dark, gloomy basement into an airy expanse. Concentrate instead on giving the room warmth and character with color, and use mirrors to increase the illusion of space and light. Strips of mirror glass set into the window reveals will make an enormous difference to the quality of light in a dark room, as does hanging a good-sized mirror on the wall facing the window, creating the illusion of a second window.

This is English-country-house decorating on a miniature scale. The narrow living room could easily feel cramped, but the combination of a large, uncurtained sash window and a striped yellow-and-cream wallpaper maximizes the feeling of light and space. The profusion of pattern in the furnishing fabrics is balanced by the tonal similarity of the colors – mellow pinks, reds and greens. The *coup de grâce* is provided by the over-sized scale of the antique tapestry.

Below right: Plain white walls and the pale cream fabric used for the curtain and upholstery confer an atmosphere of serenity and spaciousness upon this small but very smart sitting room. The L-shaped seating unit makes excellent use of the limited floor area and also allows space for a large coffee table. Below: Another, more colorful example of an L-shaped seating unit is used to create maximum seating area in the minimum space. The clear glass coffee table is less obtrusive than a solid table would be.

Below: By combining color, pattern and an over-sized piece of furniture, interior designer Michael Daly has created an atmosphere of exotic grandeur in this small living room. While of an imposing height, the depth of the tall painted cabinet is deceptively shallow so as not to protrude far into the room. A pair of *faux*-bamboo mirrors reflect light back into the room. Right: Another example of how a sizeable piece of furniture can add a sense of importance and drama to a small room.

A French marble fireplace adds architectural gravitas to this elegant living room, while an entire wall has been covered in mirror, visually to double the size of the room. The decoration of the room has been kept deliberately simple in order to increase the sense of space still further. The walls and upholstery are of a similar pale shade and just one painting hangs behind the sofa. Cushions, an oriental rug and pretty flowers add bright accents of color.

Top: This little seaside living room is barely bigger than a bath house, but it has been furnished with great charm at minimal cost. A fresh coat of white paint and seagrass floor covering are the basic requirements, followed by inexpensive, well-designed wicker armchairs, and gingham cushions. Left: Golden-yellow curtains and walls provide a plain background for the generous proportions of the furniture in this small but confidently furnished living room.

Benefiting from double-aspect windows, the size of this spacious, airy living room has been emphasized by the use of soft pastel colors typical of the eighteenth-century rococo style of decoration. Yellow, blue, taupe, pink and green harmonize against the pale cream background of the walls. The focal point of the room is a magnificent gilded console table; the well-spaced, symmetrical arrangement of pictures above takes full advantage of the generous ceiling height.

A room of this size could easily appear chilly, but the golden-yellow walls convey an atmosphere of warmth, aided and abetted by the contrasting shade of deep-pink fabric chosen for the sofa, and the rich pinks and reds of the Aubusson rug. Furnished with verve and confidence, the central part of the room is occupied by a stretch sofa. The graceful curve of the bow front with its trio of draped French windows makes a fitting backdrop for the grand piano.

The spacious, stone-flagged hallway of this old country house is used also as a sitting area. Many such houses built for the well-to-do during the sixteenth, seventeenth and eighteenth centuries have a fireplace in the hallway, but few have been made as cozy and inviting as this one. An impression of warmth is created solely by the use of red — in many shades. The fabric of the armchair and settle echo the warm pinks and reds of the large rug, while the fireside rug is a deeper red.

Color has been used sparingly in the small sitting room of this eighteenth-century cottage to create a roomy, open feeling. By keeping to the color combination of white and grey-blue an atmosphere of airy lightness is suggested; the use of the same fabric for curtains, sofa and stool reinforces the sense of simple harmony. The classical proportions of the white-painted mantelpiece are complemented by a large gilt overmantel mirror, adding to the impression of light and space.

Although every surface of this friendly living room is crammed with furniture and objects, the overall impression is one of spaciousness. The pair of wide French windows that overlook the conservatory undoubtedly contribute to this feeling. The pale uniformity of the wall color and the well-balanced arrangement of furniture impose a sense of order on an eclectic mixture of styles and fabrics. The vibrant graphic design of the rug gives the impression of elongating the room.

Display

Making the most of your possessions is an art in itself. When shown off with the swagger

and pride befitting an Old Master painting, even the humblest of everyday

objects can be transformed into a covetable treasure. Insert a

favorite photograph into an ornate frame and it will become

a source of pleasure — leaving it to molder in a drawer from one year to the next

serves no purpose whatsoever, apart from filling up valuable space.

Books are an essential feature in any living room. As well as a constant source of entertainment and

interest, their varied colors and sizes add instant warmth and character. Arranging them in rows, interspersed with

small groups of five or six volumes piled one on top of the other, can look more interesting than shelf upon shelf neatly

stacked as though part of a municipal library. Alcoves either side of a chimney are ideal for built-in bookcases.

Shelves can run from floor to ceiling, or the lower part can be designed to provide space for radiators or cupboards.

You may wish to devote some of the shelf space to a display of china or ceramics. If so,

consider fitting glass shelves. These will allow light from downlighting installed in the

ceiling to filter down, drawing attention to fine detailing and workmanship. An alternative

method of highlighting objects on glass shelves is to run strip lights behind the uprights,

providing an invisible source of illumination. As alcoves invariably seem to attract a host of electrical equipment —

television, stereo, computer, reading light and so on — remember to take this into account when drawing up an

electrical plan and if possible place the sockets in the cupboards below to hide an unsightly tangle of cables.

Shelving can be free-standing or built-in. If built-in, adding a cornice to the top will make the structure feel more part of the room. Bookcases built over the doorway make the most of every inch of space and will give added importance to the door, but they need to be designed with care if they are not to overwhelm the room. Trimming the shelves with a scalloped leather can look attractive, as can painting the interior of the shelves a contrasting color to the uprights.

In a living room lacking a fireplace, a generously proportioned bookcase placed at the center of one wall can provide an important focal point. By placing a sofa between a pair of bookcases, the balanced arrangement provides the focal point towards which furniture in other parts of the room can be directed. Utilize the wall space above the sofa to hang a large picture or mirror, or a selection of smaller pieces. A collection of china plates could provide an alternative form of decoration for the walls. While this is an accepted way of displaying traditional china and fine porcelain, the earthy reds and ochres of Mediterranean pottery look particularly effective in contemporary-style rooms.

Low-cost industrial shelving can be adapted to domestic life, especially in less formal settings. In open-plan living areas, practical steel shelving can be useful for display and storage purposes. As well as helping to divide one area from another visually, its skeletal construction means that it detracts minimally from the feeling of openness that is characteristic of loft apartments and similar spaces.

Choose the objects you wish to display with care. Have confidence in your own taste but be ruthless when it comes to selecting individual pieces. Crowding together a mass of unrelated pieces – even if each is an object of beauty – will not result in a pleasing arrangement. You don't have

to spend a fortune to find interesting items to display. Things like driftwood, stones, shells, pine cones and dried

grasses all have their decorative appeal when imaginatively arranged. Look to yourself for inspiration and analyze

why a particular object, such as a painting or a vase, gives you particular pleasure. Why not build up a collection of

related pieces in the same style? Decide which of your interests you find the most visually

rewarding. Gardening? Needlework? Travel? Cooking? It could even be

stamp collecting. Use that interest to inspire a collection of paintings

or photographs based on one of those favorite themes.

While walls are the obvious surface for displaying pictures, don't hesitate to make a

feature of a striking rug or quilt by hanging it on the wall. After all, needlework panels and

tapestries enhance the walls of many a stately home. As well as being decorative in their own right,

pictures and paintings can be used to define certain features of a room. A focal point such as a fireplace provides

the perfect backdrop for a stunning arrangement combining wall-hung art with a variety of decorative objects displayed

on the flat surface of the mantelpiece. A collection of identically framed prints or drawings becomes a focal point

when framed and mounted correctly, and can also add a sense of order when hung above a sofa or table.

Symmetry is an important factor in displaying almost anything. A pair of table lamps on a

console table or pairs of obelisks of different sizes are always more pleasing to the eye than

a single item. Similarly, wall sconces hung either side of a mirror give a balanced look to any

wall. Keeping the tops of picture frames on the same horizontal line is also a useful way of

imposing a sense of order on a perhaps otherwise irregular elevation. Hanging a painting in an unconventional position,

such as on the surface of a mirror or the uprights of bookcases, is another way to create a visual impact. Pictures come

in many forms – the only proviso being that the subject should be interesting or decorative, preferably both. If you hanker after a piece of modern art, surprise your friends and maybe yourself with your own creation. One well-known

interior designer whose apartment I visited some years ago had made his own version of a painting by a well-known

American artist. Visitors to the apartment were invariably impressed by how well the designer must have been doing to

afford to spend so much on one painting. Old Masters generally take a little longer to copy and the results will

probably be less convincing. If, however, you wish to make a feature of one particular

painting, there is no more striking way of doing this than lighting it with a concealed

projector, which throws light only onto the canvas itself without spilling over onto the

surrounding area. Although the projector itself is quite expensive, the ethereal effect of the

painting being lit from behind is second to none. If photography is an abiding interest, work on compiling a series of

portraits or landscapes that, when enlarged, will form a cohesive collection of your work. You might find that pattern

appeals more to you than pictures, so why not frame a sample of fabric or wallpaper – whether it's antique or

contemporary is purely a matter of taste.

Cushions, with all their connotations of comfort and relaxation, should play a significant part in

the decoration of the living room. The style of the room will dictate whether they are

piled high in a profusion of color and pattern or whether a more precise arrangement,

designed to coordinate with other fabrics, is called for.

When chosen with decoration in mind, the color and beauty of fresh flowers adds a welcoming flourish

to any living room. No matter how many floral patterns and motifs a room contains there is never any substitute for

the real thing, although dried and silk flowers can be effective – in moderation. Even the

smallest jug or vase filled with fresh flowers will add vitality when placed on the

mantelpiece as part of an otherwise symmetrical arrangement. Foliage and flowers in a

larger container can fill the empty void in the corner of a room.

A pair of free-standing black bookcases inset into the alcoves either side of the fireplace are filled with a well-ordered arrangement of books interspersed with decorative boxes, baskets and pictures. Above: A built-in bookcase has been incorporated into this dramatic Gothic interior to provide storage space for books, television, stereo and an unusual collection of character ceramics. Left: A floor-to-ceiling run of bookshelves frames the doorway in this country living room.

When arranged with flair and imagination, books are an effective way to add color to even the palest room. A floor-to-ceiling bookcase frames the door in this blue and cream living room. By painting the framework of the shelves in shades of blue and green to match the trompe-l'oeil panels on the walls, the bookcase has become an important part of the overall decorative scheme. The deep shelves also contain a varied collection of objects, which contributes to the general air of informality.

Below: Denise Outlaw of Arc Prints has used two classical Piranesi architectural prints with simple black frames to decorate the walls of her house. The architectural theme is continued with the stone fragments of Ionic columns displayed on the mantelpiece. Right: Art and nature in tonal harmony – a mantelpiece arrangement of clock and gilded wooden letters is enhanced by the gorgeous color and shape of these golden parrot tulips.

Above: Just the addition of a simple china pitcher filled with pencils provides a visual flourish to this austere arrangement of an antique wooden desk partnered with a modern plywood pre-formed chair. Left: In the compact Chelsea home of property developer Sara May, this unusual zinc-topped console table doubles as an occasional desk. A pair of torcheres designed by Suzanne Ruggles adds a sense of importance and order to the simple arrangement.

Balance has been imposed on this room by a collection of nine classical prints, displayed to great effect between built-in bookcases and cupboards. The close-hung symmetry of the arrangement has considerably more impact than if the prints were hung singly or in pairs. The classical theme is continued in the miscellany of objects displayed on the trunk – anatomical plaster casts, a bust and a pedimented clock. A light-hearted touch is provided by the hat-bearing cherub.

The asymmetrical layout of this airy living room is countered by the series of well-balanced arrangements. The pale cream sofa with its pair of dark paisley cushions illustrates the constant interplay of dark and light surfaces that is a feature of the decoration. A pair of tall black table lamps with pleated cream silk shades are placed at either end of the sofa to help define the seating area. The formation in which the four engravings on the far wall are hung accentuates the lofty ceiling height.

Below: The theatrical qualities of red and gold are fully exploited in this fireside arrangement in an apartment designed by Michael Daly. The uprights of the wood-grained bookcases have been stencilled in gold to suggest intricate inlay work. The bevelled mirror is flanked by smaller, more ornate brass and gilt frames. A pair of swing-arm wall lights with red and gold adds the final touch. Right: The ruddy hues of the walls, mantelpiece and wooden mirror frame are highlighted by bright green.

Above left: Warm orange walls cast a golden glow over this decorative ensemble arranged by interior designer David Hare on a nineteenth-century *rouge royale* marble mantelpiece. Framed by a tall gilded mirror the formality of the grouping is softened by the foliage of the orchid. Above: The informal arrangement of roses and mock orange adds to this mantelpiece display. The collection of portraits with its varied shapes, sizes and styles is given cohesion by being hung within a single panel.

74

Yellow walls, white dado and a strongly colored red and yellow oriental rug create an appropriately dramatic setting for this highly successful arrangement of furniture and objects of different styles. A pair of simple, provincial chairs, covered in pink *toile de Jouy,* provides a foil for the magnificence of this French commode complete with ornate gilt ornamentation. Two pretty porcelain lamps frame the table-top arrangement of a delicate gilt clock and porcelain cups and saucers.

Glass and gilt add sparkle to this carefully considered arrangement centered around a classical alabaster clock. Textural contrasts abound: the green-painted console table with its gilded decoration; pleated silk shades top the delicate glass stems of the table lamps; the neutral colors of the stone obelisks highlighted by the reflective surfaces of perspex ones; modelled forms in black of a cat, monkey and a hand add strength to this mannered and elegant collection of decorative objects.

Decorative folding screens can also have practical uses. Inspired by eighteenth-century print rooms, this three-panelled screen has been painted an earthy shade of red before being decorated with photocopies of engravings in assorted styles and sizes. As well as screening the room from the drafty hall, the folding screen adds to the visual flamboyance of this richly colored room, which is decorated in that classical combination of red and yellow.

Above left: A varied collection of furniture, sculpture, paintings and decorative objects is arranged with confidence and originality in this unpretentious living room. Every surface has been used for display but the plain white-painted walls provide a restful backdrop. Above: A colorful collection of cushions fills the gap between sofa and tapestry and adds warmth and comfort. A profusion of summer flowers and greenery in an attractive container provides the finishing touch.

Lighting

Lighting in the living room has two functions – to be decorative as well as practical. In most homes, the room is used at different times of the day for a diverse range of activities. Reading, sewing, watching television, word-processing and entertaining are some of the most usual, and the lighting requirements of each need to be taken into account if the room is to work satisfactorily from morning until night.

Flexibility is the key word to remember when it comes to deciding how the room is to be lit, and careful planning is essential if unsightly wires are to be chased into the walls, or hidden below floorboards or behind baseboards, before the room is decorated.

For the room to adapt to its multi-purpose role, install a combination of the following types of lighting.

Background or indirect lighting. Switched on from the door to provide a reasonable level of light throughout

the room.

Display or accent lighting. Focuses attention on a particular feature in the room, such as paintings, sculpture or a collection of ornaments.

Task lighting. Provides suitable light for specific activities, such as using a personal computer, watching television, reading or needlework.

Although most domestic lighting is still dependent on the conventional tungsten bulb, it's well worth familiarizing yourself with the different kinds of light sources. While the notion of fluorescent light might bring to mind any

number of unattractive institutional applications, when used sympathetically and recessed behind a pelmet or cornice, it can prove suitable for general background use, especially in a contemporary setting. Fluorescent lamps cannot be dimmed, which does tend to limit their use.

Low-voltage halogen lights are undeniably more expensive than other types of lighting but the beautiful quality of clear, white light far outweighs any disadvantages they may have. It is the closest one can get to natural daylight with an artificial light source. Low-voltage halogen lamps are now available in a wide variety of fittings – desk lights,

uplighting, downlighting and spotlights, to name but a few. One of the advantages of low-voltage lighting is the fact that any heat produced by the bulb passes through the back of the reflector. This means that the light beam is far cooler than conventional lighting – certainly a bonus if valuable paintings are being lit.

Despite their relatively short lifespan and poor energy efficiency, tungsten filament bulbs are still the most popular and widely available form of light bulb. You can buy them in a wide range of sizes and colors; with one tinted pink or yellow you can add to the impression of warmth, or to emphasize cooler colors select a pale green or blue tint. Remember that the color chosen for the walls and ceilings has an important bearing on the amount of additional light needed – while pale walls reflect light, opaque darker surfaces absorb it and stronger artificial light is required.

When shopping for light fixtures you will need to bear in mind what sort of light the

lamp will provide. You might find a particular design immensely appealing to look at, but the actual light effect it

produces could prove unsatisfactory for certain tasks. Make a study of the many different types of fittings on offer in

lighting shops before you come to a decision. By using a combination of fixtures it's possible to create a flexible

lighting system that can dramatically change the mood of the room without compromising the more functional

aspects of your lighting requirements. Single, central ceiling lights hanging from a flex do

nothing to improve a room. A chandelier is a very different matter,

especially when the level of light is controlled with a dimmer.

Other forms of ceiling lighting that adapt well to most

styles of decoration would be low-voltage downlighting and wall-washers. Downlighting

either provides general pools of light or pinpointed circles, depending on the angle of the beam

in the reflector. Wall-washers are useful if you want to highlight a collection of prints or drawings.

Spotlights can be mounted on a variety of surfaces and are adjustable: for example, they can be used to focus

attention on a particular painting or work of art. Uplighting provides an effective form of background or ambient

light by projecting a wide band of light onto the walls or ceiling, which is then reflected back into the room. By

throwing the light upwards, you emphasize the height of the room.

Unusual decorative features or displays of eye-catching objects, such as those shown

on page 84, can also benefit from the use of uplighting and wall-washers, especially when

linked to a dimmer switch.

Wall lights are available in any number of styles. Sconces can prove ideal for period-

style rooms but make sure such a light is fitted with a dimmer switch, as the bulbs are often left unshaded and the

light can appear harsh. Work or task lighting contributes enormously to making your living room an enjoyable and

relaxing setting for work and study — reading in poor light results in eye strain and a lack of concentration, just as light reflected on a computer or television screen becomes a constant source of irritation.

If the technicalities seem bewilderingly complex, think about obtaining advice from a lighting consultant. Many will

provide the initial consultation free of charge. From the many fixtures and options available they should be able to

solve any lighting problem.

The installation of new wiring should of course be undertaken before you decorate, hence the importance of working out exactly where each fixed lighting point is to be located. Once you've decided how the room is going to be arranged, work out how you wish the room to be lit, according to the time of day and its various functions. Draw a clear,

measured floorplan and elevation of each wall for your electrician, showing exactly where you wish sockets and

switches to be positioned. Don't make the mistake of underestimating the number of power points that you will need.

Extra ones are easy and inexpensive to install at the initial stages, but when added as an afterthought with surface-

mounted cable they hold little decorative appeal. At this planning stage it is important to separate the power

circuit from the lighting circuit. The lighting circuit controls those fittings such as ceiling lights and

table lamps that will be operated from the room switch. The power circuit allows for appliances

that draw more power, such as stereo equipment, vacuum cleaners and computers.

It is of course possible to give any room an instant facelift simply with the addition of one or

two well-chosen lamps. Low-voltage floor and table lights may cost rather more than the tungsten

equivalent, but when linked to a dimmer they can transform the appearance of the room. Though they are somewhat

expensive, when you decide to move on, the lights move with you. Another ploy is merely

to substitute new lampshades for tired or dated ones, making sure you resist any

temptation to play dull and safe. You could even make them yourself if you have the time

and inclination – then they are guaranteed to be original!

Unusual lamps add instant character and individuality to a room. Below: A pair of gilded wall brackets either side of this overmantel mirror would have been the conventional choice, but the startling shape of these two modern lamps bring this room right up to date. Right: modern materials and design are combined in this amusing yet practical table lamp. A highly decorative object in its own right, it provides a diffused form of background lighting.

Both these table lamps make a strong style statement. Left: Against a simple, panelled background the modern, turned wooden lampbase is well balanced by the shape and color of its parchment shade. The smooth, sculpted angles make a striking contrast teamed with an antique leather chair and a period table. Above: The gilded lamp base and plain cream shade is a perfect choice for this side table with its decorative arrangement of classical artifacts.

Below and right: Pale cream walls and matching curtains maximize the feeling of space. Superfluous decoration has been kept to a minimum in this coolly restrained classical interior. By day the room is bathed in softly suffused daylight but by night the more dramatic aspects of the room, such as the handsome pair of urns and the alcove display shelves, are brought into focus by using low-voltage halogen wall-washers, uplighting and downlighting.

The dramatic potential of this beautiful bow-fronted living room is fully exploited in the rich color scheme – deep yellow walls and curtain fabric in the same striking tones are teamed with a sofa that is covered in a strongly contrasting stripe in shades of deep red. The unusual shape of the room is echoed in the global design of the chandelier. For dining, the more intimate atmosphere created by candlelight is generally preferred.

A pair of tall lamps links the various elements in this symmetrical arrangement. A trio of decorative armorial prints, window-mounted in one frame, are illuminated from below by the lamps, which are fitted with a dimmer switch in order to regulate the level of light. The severity of this monochrome arrangement is counteracted by the bright red bunch of tulips and by the tiny flowerpots filled with roses. The strict symmetricality is also relieved by the glasses and jug.

Top: A pair of brass wall sconces balances the decorative arrangement as well as contributing to the romantic atmosphere. Stronger light comes from the parchment-shaded table lamp. Above: The tapered lines of the lamp base echo those of the carved wooden wildfowl that is displayed alongside. Left: A star-spangled lamp forms the centerpiece of this decorative table-top arrangement.

Wall-mounted swing-arm lights are excellent providers of reading light and can be used in any number of situations, doing away with the need for a surfeit of lamp-bearing, occasional tables. Positioned at a height of around 50in from the floor, they cast a good light over reading matter without glaring into the eye. In this commodious arrangement, the lights contribute to the balance of the room as well as providing light for readers sitting on the day-bed.

Above: Rosy-red walls prove an excellent backdrop for this richly colored collection of cushions. A pair of plain black lamps, fitted with decorative printed shades, is positioned on the table behind the sofa to supply general background lighting for this informal living room. Top: Chandeliers such as this simple wrought iron version can look spectacular when lit up at night with candles. Especially effective when hung above a dining table, the candle light adds to the sparkle of glass and cutlery.

This classical table lamp perfectly complements the painted decoration of the black and ochre Regency daybed. The lamp's height and handsome proportions are a prominent feature in the corner of the room and provide reading light as well as contributing a certain amount of background lighting. The plain pleated shade is the only unpatterned surface in this amusing and unconventional room with muralled walls and abundance of richly colored fabric.

Variations on a traditional theme are demonstrated in this classically simple, symmetrical arrangement of table, lamps and painting. Given a clean, pared-down contemporary feel by the use of modern materials, the black metal table and polished steel shades are in perfect harmony with the boldness of the unframed figurative work. The strength of both the color and subject matter against the white background makes a striking impression.

Directory

PAINTS

Benjamin Moore, 2501 West North Avenue, Melrose Park, IL 60160; Tel. (800) 826-2623.

Brod Dugan, 2145 Schuetz Road, St. Louis, MO 63146; Tel. (314) 567-1111.

Devoe, 4000 DuPont Circle, Louisville, KY 40207; Tel. (502) 897-9861.

Frazee, 6625, Miramar Road, San Diego, CA 92121; Tel. (619) 276-9500.

Pratt and Lambert, 75 Tonawanda Street, Buffalo, NY 14240; Tel. (716) 873-6000.

Sears, 3333 Beverly Road, Hoffman Estate, IL 60179; Tel. (800) 499-9119.

WALLPAPERS AND FABRICS

Bentley Brothers Co., 2709 South Park Road, Louisville, KY 40219; Tel. (800) 824-4777.

Brunschwig and Fills, 979 Third Avenue, New York, NY 10022; Tel. (212) 838-7878.

Calico Corners, Walnut Road Business Park, 203 Gale Lane, Kennett Square, PA 19348; Tel. (800) 777-9933.

Cowtan and Tout, 979 Third Avenue, New York, NY 10022; Tel. (212) 753-4488.

Fabric Center, 485 Electric Avenue, Fitchburg, MA 01420; Tel. (508) 343-4402.

Imperial, 23645 Mercantile Road, Beachwood, OH 44122; Tel. (216) 464-3700.

Old World Weavers, 979 Third Avenue, New York, NY 10022; Tel. (212) 355-7186.

Motif Designs, 20 Jone Street, New Rochelle, NY 10802; Tel. (800) 431-2424.

Pallas Textiles, 1330 Bellevue, Green Bay, WI 54308; Tel. (414) 468-8100.

Scalamandré, 950 Third Avenue, New York, NY 10022; Tel. (212) 980-3888.

Schumacher, 79 Madison Avenue, New York, NY 10016; Tel. (800) 552-9255.

Waverly, 79 Madison Avenue, New York, NY 10016; Tel. (800) 423-5881.

FURNITURE: CONTEMPORARY

Brown Jordan, 150 East 58th Street, New York, NY 10022; Tel. (212) 593-1390.

Hope & Wilder, 454 Broome Street, New York, NY 10013; Tel. (212) 566-9010.

IKEA, 1100 Broadway Mall, Hicksville, NY 11801; Tel. (516) 681-4532.

Knoll Group, 105 Wooster Street, New York, NY 10012; Tel. (212) 343-4000.

Kron, 1631 South Dixie Highway, Pompano Beach, FL 33060; Tel. (800) 566-5766.

Ligne Roset, 200 Lexington Avenue, New York, NY 10016; Tel. (212) 685-1099.

FURNITURE: ETHNIC

Arte de Mexico, 5505 Riverton Avenue, North Hollywood, CA 91601; Tel. (818) 769-5090.

Larry Laslo, P.O. Box 2005, High Point, NC 27261; Tel. (910) 841-3209.

Pier 1 Imports, P.O. Box 961020, Forth Worth, TX 76161-0020; Tel. (800) 447-4371.

Zona, 97 Greene Street, New York, NY 10012; Tel. (212) 925-6750.

FURNITURE: TRADITIONAL SOFAS AND CHAIRS

ABC Carpet and Home, 888 Broadway, New York, NY 10003; Tel. (212) 473-3000.

Baker, 1661 Monroe Avenue NW, Grand Rapids, MI 49505; Tel. (616) 361-7321.

Century Furniture Indutries, P.O. Box 608, Hickory, NC 28603; Tel. (800) 852-5552.

George Smith, 73 Spring Street, New York, NY 10012; Tel. (212) 226-4747.

Harden Furniture, McConnellsville, NY 13401; Tel. (315) 245-1000.

Kravet, 225 Central Avenue South, Bethpage, NY 11714; Tel. (516) 293-2000.

Lexington Furniture Co., P.O. Box 1008, Lexington, NC 27293; Tel. (704) 249-5204, Tel. (800) LEX-INFO.

Shabby Chic, 93 Greene Street, New York, NY 10012; Tel. (212) 274-9842.

Thomasville Furniture Industries, P.O. Box 339, Thomasville, NC 27361; Tel. (800) 225-0265.

Wolfman-Gold, 116 Greene Street, New York, NY 10012; Tel. (212) 431-1888.

TRADITIONAL FURNITURE AND ACCESSORIES

Ballard Designs, 1670 Defoor Avenue, NW, Atlanta, GA 30318; Tel. (404) 352-1355.

Bombay Co., P.O. Box 161009, Fort Worth, TX 76161; Tel. (800) 829-7759.

Decorators Walk, 245 Newtown Road, Plainview, NY 11803; Tel. (516) 249-3100.

English Country Antiques, P.O. Box 1995, Bridgehampton, NY 11932; Tel. (516) 537-0606.

Homestead, 223 E. Main Street, Fredericksburg, TX 78624; Tel. (210) 997-5551.

Pottery Barn, 100 North Point Street, San Francisco, CA 94109; Tel. (800) 922-5507.

Ruby Beets, P.O. Box 596, Wainscott, NY 11932; Tel. (516) 537-2802.

LIGHTING

Candella, 4863 Exposition Boulevard, Los Angeles, CA 90016; Tel. (213) 731-9811.

Cresswell, 1 Early Street, Elwood City, PA 16117; Tel. (800) 645-4172.

Halo, 400 Busse Road, Elk Grove Village, IL 60007; Tel. (708) 956-8400.

Juno, 2001 South Mt. Prospect Street, Des Plaines, IL 60017; Tel. (708) 827-9880.

FLOOR COVERINGS

ABC Carpet and Home, 888 Broadway, New York, NY 10003; Tel. (212) 473-3000.

Asmara, 451 D Street, Boston, MA 02210; Tel. (617) 261-0222.

Couristan, 2 Executive Drive, Fort Lee, NJ 07024; Tel. (800) 226-6186.

Karastan, Box 130, Eden, NC 27288; Tel. (919) 665-4000.

Michaellan and Kohlbert, 578 Broadway, New York, NY 10010; Tel. (212) 431-9009.

Rosecore, 979 Third Avenue, New York, NY 10022; Tel. (212) 421-7272.

Stark, 979 Third Avenue, New York, NY 10022; Tel. (212) 752-9000.

Thos. Woodward, 835 Madison Avenue, New York, NY 10021; Tel. (212) 988-2906.

93

ACKNOWLEDGEMENTS

The publisher should like to thank the following sources for providing the photographs for this book:

Robert Harding Picture Library/IPC Magazines 29 top, 46 left, 48 bottom, 55, 62 bottom, 66 bottom, 81 bottom/**Jan Baldwin** 6 bottom, 7 centre, 10 top, 16, 22 left, 26, 31 top, 39, 45, 50 centre, 63 centre, 64 top & centre, 65 top, 68 top, 72, top, 74, 87 top/**David Barrett** 6 centre, 12 centre & bottom, 13 centre, 21, 29 centre, 79 bottom, 89 top/**Tim Beddow** 7 bottom, 8 top, 11 middle, 13 bottom, 19 left, 27 top, 48 top, 56 bottom, 67, 81 centre/**David Brittain** 47 bottom/ **Simon Brown** 9, 27 bottom, 49 bottom, 60, 68 bottom, 77 left, 78 bottom, 87 bottom/**Richard Davies** 70/ **Christopher Drake** 12 top, 18 left, 19 right, 23 bottom, 33, 34, 42, 50 bottom, 56 top, 78 centre, 90/ **Michael Dunne** 38, 48 centre, 54 top, 71/**Clive Frost** 88/**Lu Jeffrey** 20/**Ken Kirkwood** 49 top, 91/ **Simon Lee** 10 centre, 30 centre/**Tom Leighton** 28 centre, 69 top, 87 centre, 89 bottom/**Mark Luscombe White** 36 top, 49 centre/**Nadia Mackenzie** 8 bottom, 23 top, 78 top, 79 top & middle, 82, 83 left/**John Mason** 50 top, 53 bottom/**James Merrell** 13 top, 22 right, 24, 31 centre & bottom, 43, 47 top, 59, 64 bottom, 65 centre & bottom, 66 top & centre, 76, 77 right, 80 top & bottom, 83 right, 84, 86/ **Jonathan Pilkington** 53 top, 58, 61/**Trevor Richards** 10 bottom, 14, 15, 28 bottom, 30 bottom, 41, 46 right, 81 top, 85/**Paul Ryan** 7 top & centre, 62 top & centre, 63 bottom, 73/**Andreas von Einsiedel** 11 top & bottom, 17, 18 right, 30 top, 35, 44, 51 bottom, 57, 63 top, 75/**Polly Wreford** 6 top, 28 top, 32, 36 bottom, 37.

Andreas von Einsiedel 25, 29 bottom, 40, 54 bottom, 69 bottom, 72 bottom

Christopher Wray's Lighting Emporium 80 centre

94